S0-BTT-996

Great Thoughts to Sell By

Great Thoughts to Sell By

QUOTES TO MOTIVATE YOU TO SUCCESS

Gerhard Gschwandtner

Founder and Publisher of *Selling Power*

With Photographs by Gerhard Gschwandtner

McGraw-Hill

New York Chicago San Francisco Lisbon London Madrid Mexico City Milan New Delhi San Juan Seoul Singapore Sydney Toronto

The McGraw-Hill Companies

1 2 3 4 5 6 7 8 9 0 DOC/DOC 0 9 8 7

ISBN-13: 978-0-07-147599-0
ISBN-10: 0-07-147599-0

McGraw-Hill books are available at special quantity discounts to use as premiums and sales promotions, or for use in corporate training programs. For more information, please write to the Director of Special Sales, Professional Publishing, McGraw-Hill, Two Penn Plaza, New York, NY 10121-2298. Or contact your local bookstore.

CONTENTS

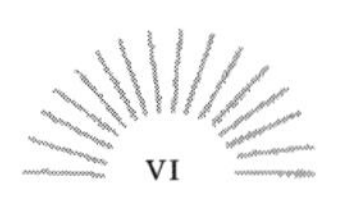

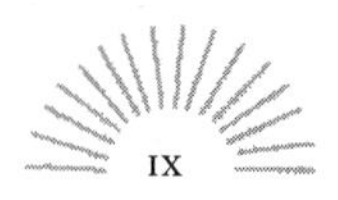

FOREWORD

From the moment we are born, we need to make sense of our world. Our ability to make sense depends on our experiences, our attitudes, and our sources of inspiration. Sometimes it is difficult to interpret reality objectively. When our emotions run high, our judgment becomes clouded. That's when a good quotation book can help.

If a customer says no, you may remind yourself that a smile is a curve that can set things straight. If you lose a sale, you may recall Napoleon Hill's saying, "Opportunity often comes disguised in the form of misfortune or temporary defeat."

In selling, every day brings new challenges, and every new challenge creates the need for insight. Without wisdom, even success can become a curse. Remember

Winston Churchill's saying, "Success is not final, failure is not fatal; it is the courage to continue that counts."

We hope that this book will offer you the courage to persevere and to transform. Think about Buckminster Fuller's insight, "There is nothing in a caterpillar that tells you it's going to be a butterfly. Stop crawling, start flying. You can use wisdom as your wings."

Gerhard Gschwandtner
Founder and Publisher, *Selling Power*

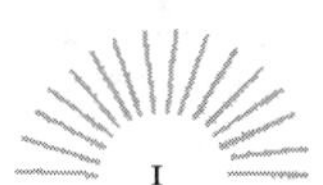

Ability

Life is like riding a bicycle.
To keep your balance you must keep moving.

—ALBERT EINSTEIN

Natural abilities are like natural plants;
they need pruning by study.

—SIR FRANCIS BACON

The question "Who ought to be boss?" is like asking
"Who ought to be the tenor in the quartet?"
Obviously, the man who can sing tenor.

—HENRY FORD

You cannot acquire experience
by making experiments.
You cannot create experience.
You must undergo it.

—ALBERT CAMUS

Action

Even if you're on the right track, you'll get run over if you just sit there.

—WILL ROGERS

Indolence is a delightful but distressing state; we must be doing something to be happy. Action is no less necessary than thought to the instinctive tendencies of the human frame.

—MOHANDAS K. GANDHI

Action may not always bring happiness; but there is no happiness without action.

—BENJAMIN DISRAELI

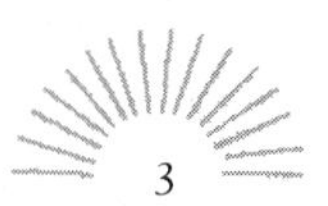

The great end of life is not knowledge but action.

—THOMAS HENRY HUXLEY

The best way out is always through.

—ROBERT FROST

It is common sense to take a method and try it. If it fails, admit it frankly and try another. But above all, try something.

—FRANKLIN D. ROOSEVELT

Periods of tranquility are seldom prolific of creative achievement. Mankind has to be stirred up.

—ALFRED NORTH WHITEHEAD

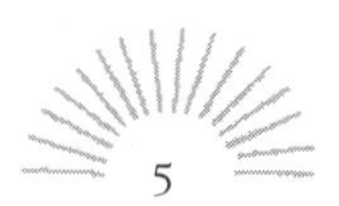

Adventure

There are two kinds of adventurers: those who go truly hoping to find adventure and those who go secretly hoping they won't.

—WILLIAM TROGDON

To the world you may be just one person, but to one person you may be the world. An adventure is only an inconvenience rightly considered. An inconvenience is an adventure wrongly considered.

—G. K. CHESTERTON

Adventure isn't hanging on a rope off the side of a mountain. Adventure is an attitude that we must apply to the day to day obstacles of life—facing new challenges, seizing new opportunities, testing our resources against the unknown and in the process, discovering our own unique potential.

—JOHN AMATT

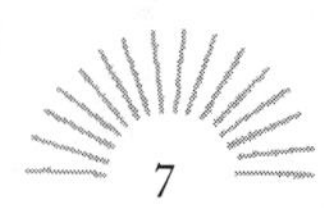

Adversity

He knows not his own strength that hath not met adversity.

—BEN JOHNSON

Challenges are what make life interesting; overcoming them is what makes life meaningful.

—JOSHUA J. MARINE

Adversity is the first path to truth.

—GEORGE GORDON (LORD) BYRON

Challenge is a dragon with a gift in its mouth … Tame the dragon and the gift is yours.

—NOELA EVANS

The harder the conflict, the more glorious the triumph. What we obtain too cheap, we esteem too lightly; it is dearness only that gives everything its value.

—THOMAS PAINE

One who gains strength by overcoming obstacles possesses the only strength which can overcome adversity.

—ALBERT SCHWEITZER

Only a loser finds it impossible to accept a temporary setback.
A winner asks why.

—ITA BUTTROSE

Problems do not go away. They must be worked through or else they remain forever a barrier to the growth and development of the spirit.

—SCOTT PECK

I love the man that can smile in trouble, that can gather strength from distress and grow brave by reflection.

—THOMAS PAINE

As we advance in life it becomes more and more difficult, but in fighting the difficulties the inmost strength of the heart is developed.

—VINCENT VAN GOGH

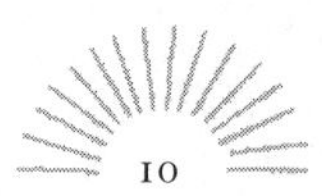

Advertising

Advertising isn't a science. It's persuasion. And persuasion is an art.

—WILLIAM BERNBACH

The spider looks for a merchant who doesn't advertise so he can spin a web across his door and lead a life of undisturbed peace.

—MARK TWAIN

Doing business without advertising is like winking at a girl in the dark. You know you're doing it, but nobody else does.

—STEUART HENDERSON BRITT

If you make a product good enough, even though you live in the depths of the forest the public will make a path to your door … But if you want the public in sufficient numbers, you would better construct a highway. Advertising is that highway.

—WILLIAM RANDOLPH HEARST

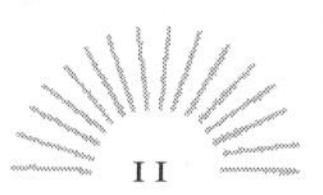

Don't sell the steak, sell the sizzle!

—ELMER WHEELER

The philosophy behind much advertising is based on the old observation that every man is really two men—the man he is and the man he wants to be.

—WILLIAM FAULKNER

In our factory, we make lipstick. In our advertising, we sell hope.

—CHARLES REVSON

Let advertisers spend the same amount of money improving their product that they do on advertising and they wouldn't have to advertise it.

—WILL ROGERS

Nothing except the mint can make money without advertising.

—THOMAS B. MACAULAY

If I were starting life all over again, I would go into the advertising business; it has risen with ever-growing rapidity to the dignity of an art.

—FRANKLIN D. ROOSEVELT

Advice

Advice is seldom welcome; and those who want it the most always like it the least.

—LORD CHESTERFIELD

I have found the best way to give advice to your children is to find out what they want and then advise them to do it.

—HARRY S TRUMAN

Advice is what we ask for when we already know the answer but wish we didn't.

—ERICA JONG

Never take the advice of someone who has not had your kind of trouble.

—SIDNEY J. HARRIS

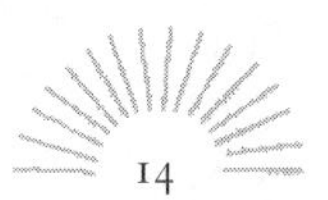

The best advice I can give is to ignore advice. Life is too short to be distracted by the opinions of others.

—RUSSELL EDSON

The advice of friends must be received with a judicious reserve; we must not give ourselves up to it and follow it blindly, whether right or wrong.

—PIERRE CHARRON

Ambition

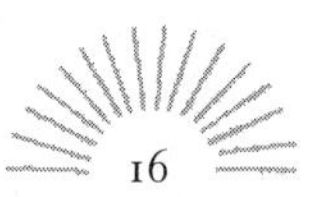

Keep away from people who try to belittle your ambitions. Small people always do that, but the really great ones make you feel that you, too, can become great.

—MARK TWAIN

First say to yourself what you would be; and then do what you have to do.

—EPICTETUS

Arrogance

Early in life I had to choose between honest arrogance and hypocritical humility. I chose honest arrogance and have seen no occasion to change.

—FRANK LLOYD WRIGHT

Arrogance diminishes wisdom.

—ARABIC PROVERB

I'm not arrogant. I just believe there's no human problem that couldn't be solved—if people would simply do as I tell them.

—DONALD REGAN

Attitude

The greatest discovery of my generation is that a human being can alter his life by altering his attitudes of mind.

—WILLIAM JAMES

A strong positive mental attitude will create more miracles than any wonder drug.

—PATRICIA NEAL

An inexhaustible good nature is one of the most precious gifts of heaven, spreading itself like oil over the troubled sea of thought, and keeping the mind smooth and equable in the roughest weather.

—WASHINGTON IRVING

No pessimist ever discovered the secret of the stars, or sailed to an uncharted land, or opened a new doorway for the human spirit.

—HELEN KELLER

Our attitude toward life determines life's attitude toward us.

—EARL NIGHTINGALE

A happy person is not a person in a certain set of circumstances, but rather a person with a certain set of attitudes.

—HUGH DOWNS

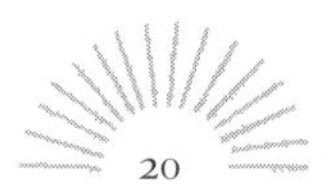

Beauty

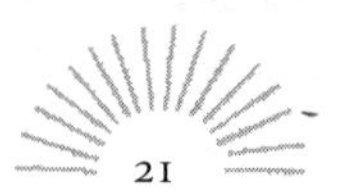

Beauty endures only for as long as it can be seen; goodness, beautiful today, will remain so tomorrow.

—SAPPHO

Think of all the beauty still left around you and be happy.

—ANNE FRANK

The excellence of every art is its intensity, capable of making all disagreeables evaporate from their being in close relationship with beauty and truth.

—JOHN KEATS

Develop interest in life as you see it; in people, things, literature, music—the world is so rich, simply throbbing with rich treasures, beautiful souls and interesting people. Forget yourself.

—HENRY MILLER

I'm tired of all this nonsense about beauty being only skin-deep. That's deep enough. What do you want, an adorable pancreas?

—JEAN KERR

Belief

Your belief determines your action and your action determines your results, but first you have to believe.

—MARK VICTOR HANSEN

The depth of your belief and the strength of your conviction determine the power of your personality.

—HENRY DAVID THOREAU

Boasting

Bragging may not bring happiness, but no man having caught a large fish goes home through an alley.

—ANONYMOUS

First do it, then say it.

—RUSSIAN PROVERB

All the extraordinary men I have ever known were chiefly extraordinary in their own estimations.

—WOODROW WILSON

It ain't braggin' if you can do it.

—DIZZY DEAN

The greatest of faults, I should say, is to be conscious of none.

—THOMAS CARLYLE

I have my faults, but being wrong ain't one of them.

—JIMMY HOFFA

Noise proves nothing. Often a hen who has merely laid an egg cackles as if she laid an asteroid.

—MARK TWAIN

Where boasting ends, there dignity begins.

—EDWARD YOUNG

Boredom

Boredom is having to listen to someone talk about himself when I want to talk about me.

—TOM PACIORSEK

Now when I bore people at a party, they think it's their fault.

—HENRY KISSINGER

The best way to be boring is to leave nothing out.

—VOLTAIRE

Half of the world is composed of people who have something to say and can't, and the other half have nothing to say and keep on saying it.

—ROBERT FROST

Budgeting

The reason most of us don't live within our income is that we don't consider that living.

—JOE MOORE

My problem lies in reconciling my gross habits with my net income.

—ERROL FLYNN

A budget tells us what we can afford but it doesn't keep us from buying it.

—WILLIAM FEATHER

About the time we can make both ends meet, somebody moves the ends.

—HERBERT HOOVER

Business

There is no time for cut-and-dried monotony. There is time for work and time for love. That leaves no other time!

—COCO CHANEL

We demand that big business give people a square deal; in return we must insist that when anyone engaged in big business honestly endeavors to do right, he shall himself be given a square deal.

—THEODORE ROOSEVELT

There's no business like show business, but there are several businesses like accounting.

—DAVID LETTERMAN

In the modern world of business, it is useless to be a creative original thinker unless you can also sell what you create. Management cannot be expected to recognize a good idea unless it is presented to them by a good salesman.

—DAVID M. OGILVY

The gambling known as business looks with austere disfavor upon the business known as gambling.

—AMBROSE BIERCE

It is truly said that a corporation has no conscience. But a corporation of conscientious men is a corporation with a conscience.

—HENRY DAVID THOREAU

Chance

In the field of observation, chance favors only the prepared mind.

—LOUIS PASTEUR

Chance is always powerful. Let your hook be always cast; in the pool where you least expect it, there will be a fish.

—OVID

Work and acquire, and thou hast chained the wheel of Chance.

—RALPH WALDO EMERSON

Change

Times change and we change with them.

—LATIN PROVERB

If you don't like something, change it. If you can't change it, change your attitude. Don't complain.

—MAYA ANGELOU

It may be hard for an egg to turn into a bird: it would be a jolly sight harder for it to learn to fly while remaining an egg. We are like eggs at present. And you cannot go on indefinitely being just an ordinary, decent egg. We must be hatched or go bad.

—C. S. LEWIS

Not everything that is faced can be changed, but nothing can be changed until it is faced.

—JAMES A. BALDWIN

We all have big changes in our lives that are more or less a second chance.

—HARRISON FORD

People do not change easily or all at once. Most of us need a chance to try out new ways and to become familiar with new procedures.

—WILLIAM G. DYER

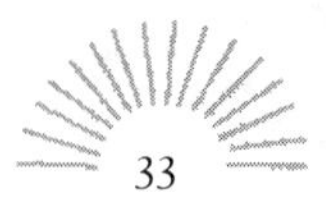

A great wind is blowing, and that gives you either imagination or a headache.

—CATHERINE THE GREAT

After you've done a thing the same way for two years, look it over carefully. After five years, look at it with suspicion. After ten years, throw it out and start over.

—ALFRED EDWARD PERLMAN

The man who never alters his opinion is like standing water and breeds reptiles of the mind.

—WILLIAM BLAKE

They always say time changes things, but you actually have to change them yourself.

—ANDY WARHOL

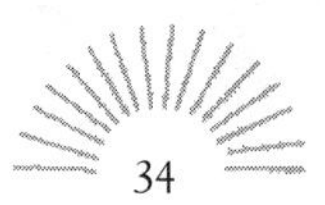

Character

The best index to a person's character is (a) how he treats people who can't do him any good and (b) how he treats people who can't fight back.

—ABIGAIL VAN BUREN

Character is what you are in the dark.

—DWIGHT L. MOODY

Start with what is right, rather than what is acceptable.

—PETER DRUCKER

Men show their characters in nothing more clearly than in what they think laughable.

—JOHANN WOLFGANG VON GOETHE

Character cannot be developed in ease and quiet. Only through experience of trial and suffering can the soul be strengthened, vision cleared, ambition inspired and success achieved.

—HELEN KELLER

Property may be destroyed and money may lose its purchasing power; but character, health, knowledge and good judgment will always be in demand under all conditions.

—ROGER BABSON

Nearly all men can stand adversity, but if you want to test a man's character, give him power.

—ABRAHAM LINCOLN

When the character of a man is not clear to you, look at his friends.

—JAPANESE PROVERB

The farther behind I leave the past, the closer I am to forging my own character.

—ISABELLE EBERHARDT

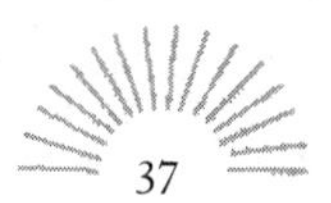

Charity

The best thing to give to your enemy is forgiveness; to an opponent, tolerance; to a friend, your heart; to your child, a good example; to a father, deference; to your mother, conduct that will make her proud of you; to yourself, respect; to all men, charity.

—FRANCIS MAITLAND BALFOUR

A bone to the dog is not charity. Charity is the bone shared with the dog, when you are just as hungry as the dog.

—JACK LONDON

Too many have dispensed with generosity in order to practice charity.

—ALBERT CAMUS

The value of a man resides in what he gives and not in what he is capable of receiving.

—ALBERT EINSTEIN

In charity there is no excess.

—SIR FRANCIS BACON

Civilization

Civilization is built on a number of ultimate principles ... respect for human life, the punishment of crimes against property and persons, the equality of all good citizens before the law ... or, in a word, justice.

—MAX NORDAU

Civilization is a method of living, an attitude of equal respect for all men.

—JANE ADDAMS

Civilization is the art of living in towns of such size that everyone does not know everyone else.

—JULIAN JAYNES

I do not believe that civilizations have to die, because civilization is not an organism. It is a product of wills.

—ARNOLD J. TOYNBEE

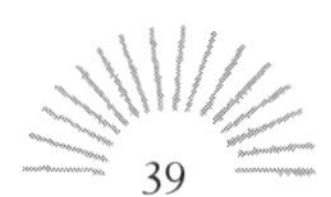

Underlying the whole scheme of civilization is the confidence men have in each other: confidence in their integrity, confidence in their honesty, confidence in their future.

—BOURKE COCKRAN

The true civilization is where every man gives to every other every right that he claims for himself.

—ROBERT INGERSOLL

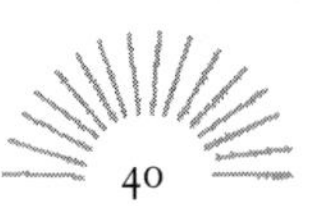

Committees

A committee is a cul-de-sac down which ideas are lured and then quietly strangled.

—SIR BARNETT COCKS

Committee—a group of men who keep minutes and waste hours.

—MILTON BERLE

Nothing is ever accomplished by committee unless it consists of three members, one of who happens to be sick and the other absent.

—HENDRIK VAN LOON

Communication

The right to be heard does not automatically include the right to be taken seriously.

—HUBERT HUMPHREY

Once a human being arrives on this earth, communication is the largest single factor determining what kinds of relationships he makes with others and what happens to him in the world about him.

—VIRGINIA SATIR

It usually takes me more than three weeks to prepare a good impromptu speech.

—MARK TWAIN

I have made this letter longer than usual, only because I have not had the time to make it shorter.

—BLAISE PASCAL

Good communication is as stimulating as black coffee, and just as hard to sleep after.

—ANNE MORROW LINDBERGH

It is ironic that in this age of electronic communications, personal interaction is becoming more important than ever.

—REGIS McKENNA

Speech is power: speech is to persuade, to convert, to compel. It is to bring another out of his bad sense into your good sense.

—RALPH WALDO EMERSON

Competition

Competition, you know, is a lot like chastity. It is widely praised, but alas, too little practiced.

—CAROL TUCKER

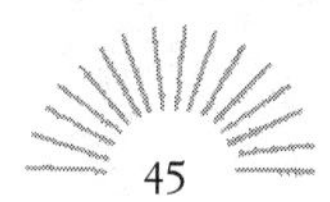

You may have to fight a battle more than once to win it.

—MARGARET THATCHER

I'm not in competition with anybody but myself. My goal is to beat my last performance.

—CELINE DION

Don't wrestle with pigs; you get dirty and they enjoy it.

—ANONYMOUS

If you watch a game, it's fun. If you play it, it's recreation. If you work at it, it's golf.

—BOB HOPE

Almost any game with any ball is a good game.

—ROBERT LYND

Computers and Technology

One machine can do the work of fifty ordinary men. No machine can do the work of one extraordinary man.

—ELBERT HUBBARD

The Internet is so big, so powerful and pointless that for some people it is a complete substitute for life.

—ANDREW BROWN

Just the other day I listened to a young fellow sing a very passionate song about how technology is killing us and all. But before he started, he bent down and plugged his electric guitar into the wall socket.

—PAUL GOODMAN

Computers are useless. They can only give you answers.

—PABLO PICASSO

Man is still the most extraordinary computer of all.

—JOHN F. KENNEDY

A computer does not substitute for judgment any more than a pencil substitutes for literacy. But writing without a pencil is no particular advantage.

—ROBERT McNAMARA

It was not so long ago that people thought that semiconductors were part-time orchestra leaders and microchips were very, very small snack foods.

—GERALDINE FERRARO

To err is human, but to really foul up requires a computer.

—PAUL EHRLICH

Confidence

Success in business requires training and discipline and hard work. But if you're not frightened by these things, the opportunities are just as great today as they ever were.

—DAVID ROCKEFELLER

Confidence is contagious. So is lack of confidence.

—VINCE LOMBARDI

If a man doesn't delight in himself and the force in him and feel that he and it are wonders, how is all life to become important to him?

—SHERWOOD ANDERSON

Every time you don't follow your inner guidance, you feel a loss of energy, loss of power, a sense of spiritual deadness.

—SHAKTI GAWAIN

Believe in yourself! Have faith in your abilities! Without a humble but reasonable confidence in your own powers you cannot be successful or happy.

—NORMAN VINCENT PEALE

Self-reliance is the only road to true freedom, and being one's own person is its ultimate reward.

—PATRICIA SAMPSON

It seems to me that people have vast potential. Most people can do extraordinary things if they have the confidence or take the risks. Yet most people don't. They sit in front of the telly and treat life as if it goes on forever.

—PHILIP ADAMS

Don't let life discourage you; everyone who got where he is had to begin where he was.

—RICHARD L. EVANS

Courage

Courage is doing what you're afraid to do. There can be no courage unless you're scared.

—EDDIE RICKENBACKER

The ultimate measure of a man is not where he stands in moments of comfort, but where he stands at times of challenge and controversy.

—MARTIN LUTHER KING JR.

Great crises produce great men and great deeds of courage.

—JOHN F. KENNEDY

Do the thing you are afraid to do, and the death of fear is certain.

—RALPH WALDO EMERSON

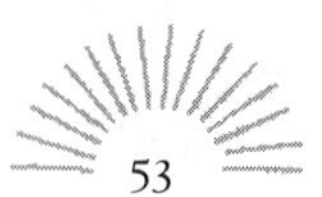

What would we be if we had no courage to attempt anything?

—VINCENT VAN GOGH

The guts carry the feet, not the feet the guts.

—MIGUEL DE CERVANTES SAAVEDRA

Courage is the ladder on which all the other virtues mount.

—CLARE BOOTHE LUCE

Creativity

Creativity can solve almost any problem. The creative act, the defeat of habit by originality, overcomes everything.

—GEORGE LOIS

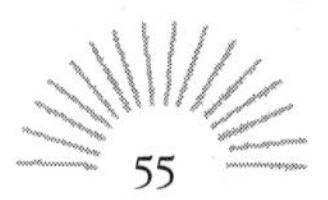

Every act of creation is first of all an act of destruction.

—PABLO PICASSO

What is now proved was once only imagined.

—WILLIAM BLAKE

Thank goodness I was never sent to school; it would have rubbed off some of the originality.

—BEATRIX POTTER

Daring ideas are like chessmen moved forward. They may be beaten, but they may start a winning game.

—JOHANN WOLFGANG VON GOETHE

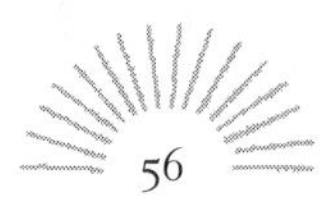

Critics

Pay no attention to what the critics say. A statue has never been erected in honor of a critic.

—JEAN SIBELIUS

To escape criticism—do nothing, say nothing, be nothing.

—ELBERT HUBBARD

Critics are like eunuchs in a harem. They know how it's done; they've seen it done every day; but they're unable to do it themselves.

—BRENDAN BEHAN

Do what you feel in your heart to be right—for you'll be criticized anyway. You'll be damned if you do, and damned if you don't.

—ELEANOR ROOSEVELT

How much easier it is to be critical than to be correct.

—BENJAMIN DISRAELI

Decision Making

If you do not know where you are going, every road will get you nowhere.

—HENRY KISSINGER

There is a syndrome in sports called "paralysis by analysis."

—ARTHUR ASHE

Make every decision as if you owned the whole company.

—ROBERT TOWNSEND

You can use all the quantitative data you can get, but you still have to distrust it and use your own intelligence and judgment.

—ALVIN TOFFLER

It is only in our decisions that we are important.

—JEAN-PAUL SARTRE

Between two evils, I always pick the one I never tried before.

—MAE WEST

Take time to deliberate, but when the time for action arrives, stop thinking and go in.

—ANDREW JACKSON

Not to decide is to decide.

—HARVEY COX

Diligence

I studied the lives of great men and famous women, and I found that the men and women who got to the top were those who did the jobs they had in hand, with everything they had of energy and enthusiasm.

—HARRY S TRUMAN

Plough deep while sluggards sleep.

—BENJAMIN FRANKLIN

Everything comes to him who hustles while he waits.

—THOMAS EDISON

Look at a day when you are supremely satisfied at the end. It's not a day when you lounge around doing nothing; it's when you've had everything to do, and you've done it.

—MARGARET THATCHER

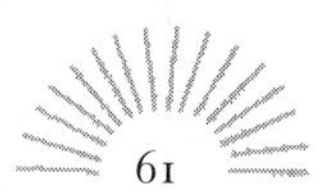

Always bear in mind that your own resolution to succeed is more important than any other one thing.

—ABRAHAM LINCOLN

Heights by great men reached and kept were not obtained by sudden flight but, while their companions slept, they were toiling upward in the night.

—HENRY WADSWORTH LONGFELLOW

The highest reward for person's toil is not what they get for it, but what they become by it.

—JOHN RUSKIN

Discovery

There is no top. There are always further heights to reach.

—JASCHA HEIFETZ

Discovery consists of seeing what everybody has seen and thinking what nobody has thought.

—ALBERT VON SZENT-GYORGYI

The beginning of knowledge is the discovery of something we do not understand.

—FRANK HERBERT

The real voyage of discovery consists not in making new landscapes but in having new eyes.

—MARCEL PROUST

Dreams

Think "impossible" and dreams get discarded, projects get abandoned, and hope for wellness is torpedoed. But let someone yell the words "It's possible," and resources we hadn't been aware of come rushing in to assist us in our quest.

—GREG ANDERSON

When our memories outweigh our dreams, we have grown old.

—WILLIAM J. (BILL) CLINTON

Sometimes dreams alter the course of an entire life.

—JUDITH DUERK

Don't be afraid of the space between your dreams and reality. If you can dream it, you can make it so.

—BELVA DAVIS

If one advances in the direction of his dreams, one will meet with success unexpected in common hours.

—HENRY DAVID THOREAU

To accomplish great things, we must dream as well as act.

—ANATOLE FRANCE

Cherish your vision and your dreams as they are the children of your soul, the blueprints of your ultimate achievements.

—NAPOLEON HILL

All people dream, but not equally. Those who dream by night in the dusty recesses of their mind, wake in the morning to find that it was vanity. But the dreamers of the day are dangerous people, for they dream their dreams with open eyes, and make them come true.

—T. E. LAWRENCE (LAWRENCE OF ARABIA)

Dreaming permits each and every one of us to be quietly and safely insane every night of our lives.

—WILLIAM DEMENT

Your hopes, dreams and aspirations are legitimate. They are trying to take you airborne, above the clouds—above the storms—if you only let them.

—WILLIAM JAMES

Education

Education's purpose is to replace an empty mind with an open one.

—MALCOLM FORBES

It is possible to store the mind with a million facts and still be entirely uneducated.

—ALEC BOURNE

There is nothing so stupid as the educated man if you get him off the thing he was educated in.

—WILL ROGERS

Good teaching is one-fourth preparation and three-fourths theater.

—GAIL GODWIN

She knows what is the best purpose of education: not to be frightened by the best but to treat it as part of daily life.

—JOHN MASON BROWN

Enthusiasm

Enthusiasm is contagious. Be a carrier.

—SUSAN RABIN

Enthusiasm spells the difference between mediocrity and accomplishment.

—NORMAN VINCENT PEALE

Energy is the one power that drives every human being. It is not lost by exertion but maintained by it, for it is a faculty of the psyche.

—GERMAINE GREER

You will do foolish things, but do them with enthusiasm.

—COLLETTE

If you aren't fired with enthusiasm, you will be fired with enthusiasm.

—VINCE LOMBARDI

Life's blows cannot break a person whose spirit is warmed at the fire of enthusiasm.

—NORMAN VINCENT PEALE

Enterprise

Self-made men are always apt to be a little too proud of the job.

—JOSH BILLINGS

What would we be if we had no courage to attempt anything?

—VINCENT VAN GOGH

Never follow the crowd.

—BERNARD BARUCH

Unless you enter the tiger's den, you cannot take the cubs.

—JAPANESE PROVERB

Ethics

Relativity applies to physics, not ethics.

—ALBERT EINSTEIN

Those who stand for nothing fall for anything.

—ALEXANDER HAMILTON

Conscience is the inner voice that warns us that someone may be looking.

—H. L. MENCKEN

It is in times of difficulty that great nations, like great men, display the whole energy of their character and become an object of admiration to posterity.

—NAPOLEON BONAPARTE

Always do right. This will gratify some people and astonish the rest.

—MARK TWAIN

I would rather be the man who bought the Brooklyn Bridge, than the one who sold it.

—WILL ROGERS

Etiquette

Cleanliness and order are not matters of instinct; they are matters of education, and like most great things, you must cultivate a taste for them.

—BENJAMIN DISRAELI

Good manners will open doors that the best education cannot.

—CLARENCE THOMAS

Rudeness is the weak man's imitation of strength.

—ERIC HOFFER

Excellence

We do not act rightly because we have virtue or excellence, but we rather have those because we have acted rightly. We are what we repeatedly do. Excellence, then, is not an act but a habit.

—ARISTOTLE

It's not what you take but what you leave behind that defines greatness.

—EDWARD GARDNER

No man ever yet became great through imitation.

—SAMUEL JOHNSON

If a man has good corn or wood or boards or pigs to sell, or can make better chairs or knives, crucibles or church organs than anybody else, you will find a broad, hard-beaten road to his house, though it be in the woods.

—RALPH WALDO EMERSON

Excellence is doing ordinary things extraordinarily well.

—JOHN W. GARDNER

Greatness be nothing unless it be lasting.

—NAPOLEON BONAPARTE

Experience

The hardest thing to learn in life is which bridge to cross and which to burn.

—DAVID RUSSELL

Good judgment comes from experience, and experience comes from bad judgment.

—BARRY LePATNER

When a person with experience meets a person with money, the person with experience will get the money. And the person with money will get some experience.

—LEONARD LAUDER

Experience teaches slowly and at the cost of mistakes.

—JAMES A. FROUDE

Experience is the name everyone gives to their mistakes.

—OSCAR WILDE

Experience is that marvelous thing that enables you to recognize a mistake when you make it again.

—FRANKLIN P. JONES

Failure

Only those who dare to fail greatly can ever achieve greatly.

—ROBERT F. KENNEDY

The majority of men meet with failure because of their lack of persistence in creating new plans to take the place of those which fail.

—NAPOLEON HILL

Success is the ability to go from one failure to another with no loss of enthusiasm.

—SIR WINSTON CHURCHILL

Success isn't permanent, and failure isn't fatal.

—MIKE DITKA

If at first you don't succeed, try, try again. Then quit. There's no use being a damn fool about it.

—W. C. FIELDS

About the worst thing you can say about a man is that he means well.

—HARRY S TRUMAN

I don't know the key to success, but the key to failure is trying to please everybody.

—BILL COSBY

Freedom

My definition of a free society is a society where it is safe to be unpopular.

—ADLAI E. STEVENSON JR.

Everything that is really great and inspiring is created by the individual who can labor in freedom.

—ALBERT EINSTEIN

Freedom is just chaos, with better lighting.

—ALAN DEAN FOSTER

If you want to be free, there is but one way; it is to guarantee an equally full measure of liberty to all your neighbors. There is no other.

—CARL SCHURZ

Freedom is what you do with what's been done to you.

—JEAN-PAUL SARTRE

They that can give up essential liberty to obtain a little temporary safety deserve neither liberty nor safety.

—BENJAMIN FRANKLIN

To know what you prefer instead of humbly saying Amen to what the world tells you you ought to prefer, is to have kept your soul alive.

—ROBERT LOUIS STEVENSON

Forgiveness

Forgiveness is almost a selfish act because of its immense benefits to the one who forgives.

—LAWANA BLACKWELL

The weak can never forgive. Forgiveness is the attribute of the strong.

—MOHANDAS K. GANDHI

Always forgive your enemies—nothing annoys them so much.

—OSCAR WILDE

Forgive your enemies, but never forget their names.

—JOHN F. KENNEDY

Goals

Ah, but a man's reach should exceed his grasp—or what's a heaven for?

—ROBERT BROWNING

In the long run, men hit only what they aim at. Therefore, though they should fail immediately, they had better aim at something high.

—HENRY DAVID THOREAU

Keep away from people who try to belittle your ambitions. Small people always do that, but the really great ones make you feel that you, too, can become great.

—MARK TWAIN

I feel that the greatest reward for doing is the opportunity to do more.

—JONAS SALK

Management by objectives works if you know the objectives.
Ninety percent of the time you don't.

—PETER DRUCKER

Everyone is trying to accomplish something big, not realizing that life is made up of little things.

—FRANK A. CLARK

Once you say you are going to settle for second, that's what happens to you in life, I find.

—JOHN F. KENNEDY

Goals are the fuel in the furnace of achievement.

—BRIAN TRACY

One cannot collect all the beautiful shells on the beach.

—ANNE MORROW LINDBERGH

If you chase two rabbits, both will escape.

—ANONYMOUS

Happiness

I am still determined to be cheerful and happy, in whatever situation I may be; for I have also learned from experience that the greater part of our happiness or misery depends upon our dispositions, and not upon our circumstances.

—MARTHA WASHINGTON

You will never be happier than you expect. To change your happiness, change your expectation.

—BETTE DAVIS

Success is not the key to happiness. Happiness is the key to success. If you love what you are doing, you will be successful.

—ALBERT SCHWEITZER

This very moment is a seed from which the flowers of tomorrow's happiness grow.

—MARGARET LINDSEY

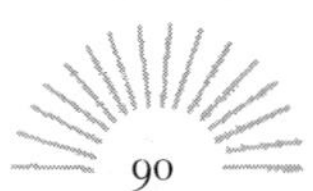

All explorers are seeking something they have lost. It is seldom that they find it and more seldom still that the attainment brings them greater happiness than the quest.

—ARTHUR C. CLARKE

One of the indictments of civilizations is that happiness and intelligence are so rarely found in the same person.

—WILLIAM FEATHER

Happiness consists more in small conveniences or pleasures that occur every day than in great pieces of good fortune that happen but seldom to a man in the course of his life.

—BENJAMIN FRANKLIN

There is no happiness in having or in getting, but only in giving.

—HENRY DRUMMOND

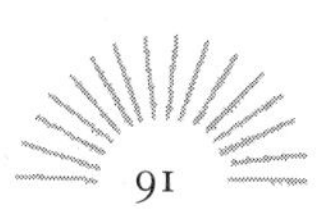

Hope

Hope is the companion of power and the mother of success, for those of us who hope strongest have within us the gift of miracles.

—SYDNEY BREMER

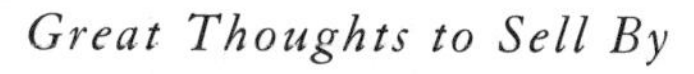

Everything that enlarges the sphere of human powers, that shows man he can do what he thought he could not do, is valuable.

—SAMUEL JOHNSON

There is nothing that fear and hope does not permit men to do.

—MARQUIS DE VAUVENARGUES

There are no hopeless situations; there are only men who have grown hopeless about them.

—CLARE BOOTHE LUCE

Humor

You can turn painful situations around through laughter. If you can find humor in anything, even poverty, you can survive it.

—BILL COSBY

Analyzing humor is like dissecting a frog. Few people are interested and the frog dies of it.

—E. B. WHITE

Humor does not include sarcasm, invalid irony, sardonicism, innuendo, or any other form of cruelty. When these things are raised to a high point they can become wit, but unlike the French and the English, we have not been much good at wit since the days of Benjamin Franklin.

—JAMES THURBER

Imagination

It is not enough to have a good mind. The main thing is to use it well.

—RENÉ DESCARTES

The simple joy of taking an idea into one's own hands and giving it proper form—that's exciting.

—GEORGE NELSON

The mind, once expanded to the dimensions of larger ideas, never returns to its original size.

—OLIVER WENDELL HOLMES

To know is nothing at all; to imagine is everything.

—ANATOLE FRANCE

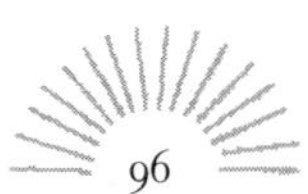

Ideas are like stars; you will not touch them with your hands.

—CARL SCHURZ

So you see, imagination needs moodling—long, inefficient, happy idling, dawdling and puttering.

—BRENDA UELAND

Imagination is more important than knowledge.

—ALBERT EINSTEIN

Individuality

It were not best that we should all think alike; it is difference of opinion that makes horse races.

—MARK TWAIN

Anybody who is any good is different from anybody else.

—FELIX FRANKFURTER

If a man does not keep pace with his companions, perhaps it is because he hears a different drummer. Let him step to the music he hears, however measured or far away.

—HENRY DAVID THOREAU

Men are born equal, but they are also born different.

—ERICH FROMM

There is only one success—to be able to spend your life in your own way.

—CHRISTOPHER MORLEY

He who reigns within himself and rules his passions, desires, and fears is more than a king.

—JOHN MILTON

We are what we pretend to be, so we must be careful what we pretend to be.

—KURT VONNEGUT

Love yourself first and everything else falls into line. You really have to love yourself to get anything done in this world.

—LUCILLE BALL

Innovation

All truths are easy to understand once they are discovered; the point is to discover them.

—GALILEO GALILEI

In differentiation, not in uniformity, lies the path of progress.

—LOUIS D. BRANDEIS

Innovation … endows resources with a new capacity to create wealth.

—PETER DRUCKER

Invention breeds invention.

—RALPH WALDO EMERSON

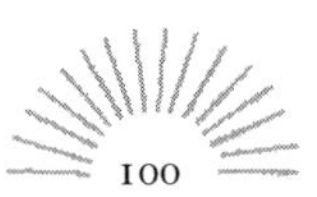

Judgment

Competence, like truth, beauty and contact lenses, is in the eye of the beholder.

—LAURENCE J. PETER AND RAYMOND HULL

It is with our judgments as with our watches; no two go just alike, yet each believes his own.

—ALEXANDER POPE

One cool judgment is worth a thousand hasty councils. The thing is to supply light and not heat.

—WOODROW WILSON

Knowledge

Today knowledge has power. It controls access to opportunity and advancement.

—PETER DRUCKER

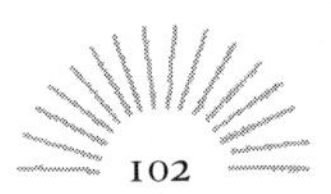

To be conscious that you are ignorant is a great step toward knowledge.

—BENJAMIN DISRAELI

The brain that doesn't feed itself eats itself.

—GORE VIDAL

The human mind is like an umbrella—it functions best when open.

—WALTER GROPIUS

Genius is an infinite capacity for taking life by the scruff of the neck.

—CHRISTOPHER QUILL

Genius is the capacity for productive reaction against one's training.

—BERNARD BERENSON

Laughter

Laughter gives us distance. It allows us to step back from an event, deal with it and then move on.

—BOB NEWHART

Laughter and tears may not persuade, but they cannot be refuted.

—MASON COOLEY

Laugh at yourself first, before anyone else can.

—ELSA MAXWELL

The human race has one really effective weapon, and that is laughter.

—MARK TWAIN

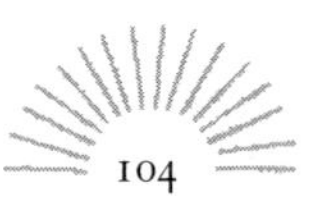

Laughter is inner jogging.

—NORMAN COUSINS

Laughter is the closet distance between two people.

—VICTOR BORGE

The most wasted of all days is one without laughter.

—E. E. CUMMINGS

Leadership

I suppose leadership at one time meant muscles; but today it means getting along with people.

—INDIRA GANDHI

If your actions create a legacy that inspires others to dream more, learn more, do more and become more, then you are an excellent leader.

—DOLLY PARTON

You do not lead by hitting people over the head—that's assault, not leadership.

—DWIGHT D. EISENHOWER

A leader has the vision and conviction that a dream can be achieved. He inspires the power and energy to get it done.

—RALPH LAUREN

Example has more followers than reason. We unconsciously imitate what pleases us and approximate to the characters we most admire.

—CHRISTIAN NEVELL BOVEE

People prefer to follow those who help them, not those who intimidate them.

—C. GENE WILKES

The final test of leadership is that he leaves behind in other men the conviction and the will to carry on.

—WALTER LIPPMANN

The leader must know, must know that he knows, and must be able to make it abundantly clear to those about him that he knows.

—CLARENCE A. RANDALL

Leadership is doing what is right when no one is watching.

—GEORGE VAN VALKENBURG

The very essence of leadership is that you have to have vision. You can't blow an uncertain trumpet.

—THEODORE HESBURGH

Learning

Learning is not attained by chance, it must be sought for with ardor and attended to with diligence.

—ABIGAIL ADAMS

Never seem more learned than the people you are with. Wear your learning like a pocket watch and keep it hidden. Do not pull it out to count the hours, but give the time when you are asked.

—LORD CHESTERFIELD

Learn from yesterday, live for today, hope for tomorrow. The important thing is to not stop questioning.

—ALBERT EINSTEIN

More can be learned from what works than from what fails.

—RENÉ DUBOIS

Listening

No man would listen to you talk if he didn't know it was his turn next.

—ED HOWE

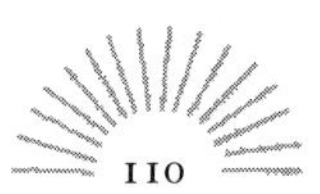

Once you get people laughing, they're listening, and you can tell them almost anything.

—HERBERT GARDNER

A good listener is not only popular everywhere, but after a while he knows something.

—WILSON MIZNER

One of the best ways to persuade others is with your ears—by listening to them.

—DEAN RUSK

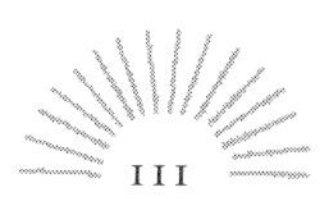

III

Luck

I've found that luck is quite predictable. If you want more luck, take more chances. Be more active. Show up more often.

—BRIAN TRACY

Luck is a dividend of sweat. The more you sweat, the luckier you get.

—RAY KROC

I'm a great believer in luck, and I find the harder I work, the more I have of it.

—STEPHEN LEACOCK

Luck is not something you can mention in the presence of self-made men.

—E. B. WHITE

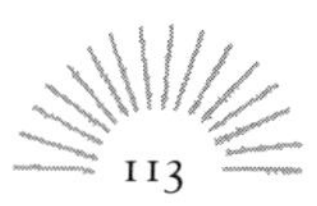

Management

As a manager the important thing is not what happens when you are there,
but what happens when you are not there.

—KENNETH H. BLANCHARD

Once somebody asked me to identify the single most useful management technique that I learned through my years of managing. My answer was "The practice of regularly scheduled one-on-one meetings."

—ANDREW S. GROVE

Lots of folks confuse bad management with destiny.

—KIN HUBBARD

The best executive is the one who has sense enough to pick good men to do what he wants done, and self-restraint enough to keep from meddling with them while they do it.

—THEODORE ROOSEVELT

Work is of two kinds: first, altering the position of matter at or near the earth's surface relative to other matter; second, telling other people to do so.

—BERTRAND RUSSELL

There are those who work all day, those who dream all day, and those who spend an hour dreaming before setting to work to fulfill those dreams. Go into the third category because there's virtually no competition.

—STEVEN J. ROSS

Any company … needs a strong, unifying sense of direction. But that need is particularly strong in an organization in which tasks are differentiated and responsibilities dispersed.

—CHRISTOPHER A. BARTLETT

To be a good shepherd is to shear the flock, not skin it!

—TIBERIUS CAESAR

Marketing

Never treat your audience as customers, always as partners.

—JIMMY STEWART

If I had my life to live over again, I would elect to be a trader of goods rather than a student of science. I think barter is a noble thing.

—ALBERT EINSTEIN

Benjamin Franklin may have discovered electricity, but it was the man who invented the meter who made the money.

—EARL WILSON

In an era of relationship marketing, sales excellence is demonstrated by the number of customers who make a second purchase.

—LOUIS E. BOONE

Mistakes

Our greatest glory is not in never failing, but in rising up every time we fail.

—RALPH WALDO EMERSON

Failure is only the opportunity to begin again more intelligently.

—HENRY FORD

A person who never made a mistake never tried anything new.

—ALBERT EINSTEIN

All the mistakes I ever made were when I wanted to say "No" and said "Yes."

—MOSS HART

Trust your instincts. Your mistakes might as well be your own instead of someone else's.

—BILLY WILDER

Morality

A truth that's told with bad intent beats all the lies you can invent.

—WILLIAM BLAKE

What is morality in any given time or place? It is what the majority then and there happen to like and immorality is what they dislike.

—ALFRED NORTH WHITEHEAD

What is moral is what you feel good after.

—ERNEST HEMINGWAY

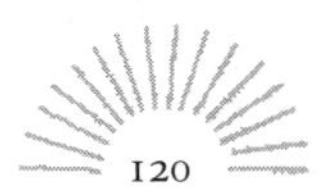

Motivation

I have yet to find the man, however exalted his station, who did not do better work and put forth greater effort under a spirit of approval than under a spirit of criticism.

—CHARLES SCHWAB

A person usually has two reasons for doing something: a good reason and a real reason.

—JOHN PIERPONT MORGAN

Winning isn't everything. Wanting to win is.

—CATFISH HUNTER

Motivation is like food for the brain. You cannot get enough in one sitting. It needs continual and regular top-ups.

—PETER DAVIES

All progress is based upon a universal, innate desire on the part of every living organism to live beyond its income.

—SAMUEL BUTLER

You can't push anyone up the ladder unless he is willing to climb himself.

—ANDREW CARNEGIE

No man does anything from a single motive.

—SAMUEL TAYLOR COLERIDGE

Always in a moment of extreme danger things can be done which had previously been thought impossible.

—GENERAL IRWIN ROMMEL

Where the willingness is great, the difficulties cannot be great.

—NICCOLÒ MACHIAVELLI

Nature

Nature is not only all that is visible to the eye, it also includes the inner pictures of the soul.

—EDVARD MUNCH

The first snow had not long fallen, and all nature was under the spell of the fresh snow.

—ANTON CHEKHOV

A woodland in full color is awesome as a forest fire, in magnitude at least, but a single tree is like a dancing tongue of flame to warm the heart.

—HAL BORLAND

To sit in the shade on a fine day and look upon verdure is the most perfect refreshment.

—JANE AUSTEN

One of the most tragic things I know about human nature is that all of us tend to put off living. We are all dreaming of some magical rose garden over the horizon instead of enjoying the roses that are blooming outside our windows today.

—DALE CARNEGIE

Opinions

Be still when you have nothing to say; when genuine passion moves you, say what you've got to say, and say it hot.

—D. H. LAWRENCE

To hold the same views at forty as we held at twenty is to have been stupefied for a score of years and to take rank, not as a prophet, but as an unteachable brat, well birched and none the wiser.

—ROBERT LOUIS STEVENSON

The easiest thing to be in the world is you. The most difficult thing to be is what other people want you to be. Don't let them put you in that position.

—LEO BUSCAGLIA

Opportunity

Problems can become opportunities when the right people get together.

—ROBERT REDFORD

Small opportunities are often the beginning of great enterprises.

—DEMOSTHENES

This time, like all times, is a very good one if we but know what to do with it.

—RALPH WALDO EMERSON

A wise man will make more opportunities than he finds.

—SIR FRANCIS BACON

If opportunity doesn't knock, build a door.

—MILTON BERLE

Opportunity is missed by most people because it comes dressed in overalls and looks like work.

—THOMAS EDISON

Too many people are thinking of security instead of opportunity. They seem to be more afraid of life than death.

—JAMES F. BYMES

There will come a time when big opportunities will be presented to you, and you've got to be in a position to take advantage of them.

—SAM WALTON

Optimism

Two men look out through the same bars: One sees the mud, and one the stars.

—FREDERICK LANGBRIDGE

A pessimist is one who makes difficulties of his opportunities; an optimist is one who makes opportunities of his difficulties.

—REGINALD B. MANSELL

I am optimistic and confident in all that I do. I affirm only the best for myself and others. I am the creator of my life and my world. I meet daily challenges gracefully and with complete confidence. I fill my mind with positive, nurturing, and healing thoughts.

—ALICE POTTER

Positiveness is a good quality for preachers and speakers, because whoever shares his thoughts with the public will convince them as he himself appears convinced.

—JONATHAN SWIFT

Passion

Only passions, great passions, can elevate the soul to great things.

—DENIS DIDEROT

One person with passion is better than forty people merely interested.

—E. M. FORSTER

I swing big, with everything I got. I hit big or I miss big. I like to hit as big as I can.

—BABE RUTH

It's the talent and passion that count in success.

—INGRID BERGMAN

Peace

For it isn't enough to talk about peace. One must believe in it. And it isn't enough to believe in it. One must work at it.

—ELEANOR ROOSEVELT

The world will never have lasting peace so long as men reserve for war the finest human qualities. Peace, no less than war, requires idealism and self-sacrifice and a righteous and dynamic faith.

—JOHN FOSTER DULLES

Peace can endure only so long as humanity really insists upon it, and is willing to work for it and sacrifice for it.

—FRANKLIN D. ROOSEVELT

People

You can dream, create, design, and build the most wonderful place in the world, but it requires people to make the dream a reality.

—WALT DISNEY

Individually, we are one drop. Together, we are an ocean.

—RYUNOSUKE SATORO

Hire the best people and then delegate.

—CAROL A. TABER

Treat employees like partners, and they act like partners.

—FRED ALLEN, CHAIRMAN OF PITNEY-BOWES CO.

Two things are infinite: the universe and human stupidity; and I'm not sure about the universe.

—ALBERT EINSTEIN

Performance

It is immutable law in business that words are words, explanations are explanations, promises are promises, but only performance is reality.

—HAROLD S. GENEEN

We should not judge a man's merits by his qualities, but by the use he makes of them.

—FRANÇOIS DE LA ROCHEFOUCAULD

Only a mediocre person is always at his best.

—LAURENCE J. PETER

We expect more from ourselves than we have any right to by virtue of our endowments.

—OLIVER WENDELL HOLMES

It is possible to be a sage in some things and a child in others, to be at once ferocious and retarded, shrewd and foolish, serene and irritable.

—WALTER LIPPMANN

It is not good to be better than the very worst.

—SENECA

Perseverance

Patience and perseverance have a magical effect before which difficulties disappear and obstacles vanish.

—JOHN QUINCY ADAMS

Most people give up just when they're about to achieve success. They quit on the one-yard line. They give up at the last minute of the game, one foot from a winning touchdown.

—H. ROSS PEROT

Permanence, perseverance and persistence in spite of all obstacles, discouragements, and impossibilities: It is this that in all things distinguishes the strong soul from the weak.

—THOMAS CARLYLE

Through perseverance many people win success out of what seemed destined to be certain failure.

—BENJAMIN DISRAELI

Perseverance is not a long race; it is many short races one after another.

—WALTER ELLIOTT

In the confrontation between the stream and the rock, the stream always wins—not through strength but by perseverance.

—H. JACKSON BROWN

There is no royal road to anything. One thing at a time … all things in succession. That which grows fast withers as rapidly; that which grows slowly endures.

—J. G. HOLLAND

With ordinary talents and extraordinary perseverance, all things are attainable.

—SIR THOMAS FOWELL BUXTON

A champion is one who gets up when he can't.

—JACK DEMPSEY

Persuasion

He who has truth at his heart need never fear the want of persuasion on his tongue.

—JOHN RUSKIN

He who wants to persuade should put his trust not in the right argument, but in the right word. The power of sound has always been greater than the power of sense.

—JOSEPH CONRAD

People's minds are changed through observation and not through argument.

—WILL ROGERS

The mind is no match with the heart in persuasion; constitutionality is no match with compassion.

—EVERETT M. DIRKSEN

In a republican nation whose citizens are to be led by reason and persuasion and not by force, the art of reasoning becomes of first importance.

—THOMAS JEFFERSON

There are three kinds of lies: lies, damn lies, and statistics.

—BENJAMIN DISRAELI

Planning

If you have built castles in the air, your work need not be lost. That is where they should be. Now put the foundation under them.

—HENRY DAVID THOREAU

Nothing is particularly hard if you divide it into small jobs.

—HENRY FORD

You've got to think about big things while you're doing small things, so that all the small things go in the right direction.

—ALVIN TOFFLER

Any plan is bad which is not susceptible to change.

—BARTOLOMEO DA SAN CONCORDIO

Planning is an unnatural process; it is much more fun to do something.

—SIR JOHN HARVEY-JONES

Victory often goes to the army that makes the least mistakes, not the most brilliant plans.

—CHARLES DE GAULLE

Plans are nothing; planning is everything.

—DWIGHT D. EISENHOWER

Some people are making such thorough preparation for rainy days that they aren't enjoying today's sunshine.

—WILLIAM FEATHER

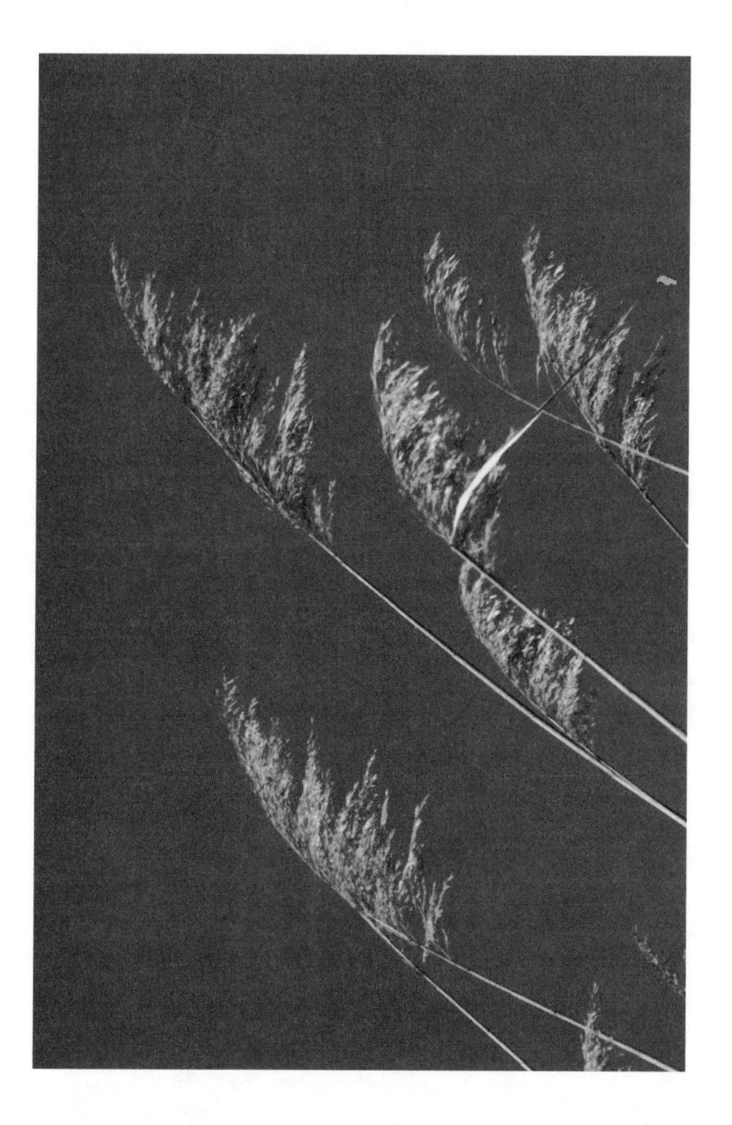

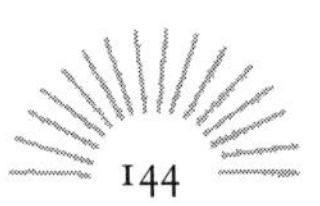

Politics

Ninety percent of the politicians give the other 10 percent a bad reputation.

—HENRY KISSINGER

A politician is a person with whose politics you don't agree; if you agree with him, he is a statesman.

—DAVID LLOYD GEORGE

Politicians are the same all over. They promise to build a bridge even where there is no river.

—NIKITA KHRUSHCHEV

Politics is not the art of the possible. It consists in choosing between the disastrous and the unpalatable.

—JOHN KENNETH GALBRAITH

Politics is supposed to be the second oldest profession. I have come to realize that it bears a very close resemblance to the first.

—RONALD REAGAN

The purification of politics is an iridescent dream.

—JOHN JAMES INGALLS

Praise

Sandwich every bit of criticism between two heavy layers of praise.

—MARY KAY ASH

When someone does something good, applaud! You will make two people happy.

—SAMUEL GOLDWYN

I praise loudly; I blame softly.

—CATHERINE THE GREAT

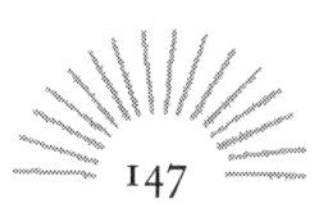

It's always worthwhile to make others aware of their worth.

—MALCOLM FORBES

Predictions

To predict the future, we need logic; but we also need faith and imagination, which can sometimes defy logic itself.

—ARTHUR C. CLARKE

Trying to predict the future is like trying to drive down a country road at night with no lights while looking out the back window.

—PETER DRUCKER

It is always wise to look ahead, but difficult to look further than you can see.

—SIR WINSTON CHURCHILL

The art of prophecy is very difficult, especially with respect to the future.

—MARK TWAIN

He can't last. I tell you flatly, he can't last.

—JACKIE GLEASON ON ELVIS PRESLEY

Problem Solving

A problem well stated is a problem half solved.

—CHARLES F. KETTERING

Never tell people how to do things. Tell them what to do, and they will surprise you with their ingenuity.

—GEORGE S. PATTON

Problems are only opportunities in work clothes.

—HENRY J. KAISER

It isn't that they can't see the solution, it's that they can't see the problem.

—G. K. CHESTERTON

Divide each difficulty into as many parts as is feasible and necessary to resolve it.

—RENÉ DESCARTES

Men are never so likely to settle a question rightly as when they discuss it freely.

—THOMAS B. MACAULAY

For every complex problem, there is a solution that is simple, neat and wrong.

—H. L. MENCKEN

The direct use of force is such a poor solution to any problem—it is generally employed only by small children and large nations.

—DAVID FRIEDMAN

Product

Anything that won't sell, I don't want to invent. Its sale is proof of utility, and utility is success.

—THOMAS EDISON

When the product is right, you don't have to be a great marketer.

—LEE IACOCCA

Before you build a better mousetrap, it helps to know if there are any mice out there.

—MORTIMER B. ZUCKERMAN

A company with a good product rarely needs a mission statement.

—SCOTT ADAMS

Progress

We may affirm that nothing great in the world has been accomplished without passion.

—GEORG W. F. HEGEL

There is nothing more difficult … than to take the lead in the introduction of a new order of things.

—NICCOLÒ MACHIAVELLI

Obstacles are things a person sees when he takes his eyes off his goal.

—E. JOSEPH COSSMAN

Purpose

You are a child of the Universe, no less than the moon and the stars; you have a right to be here. And whether or not it is clear to you, no doubt the Universe is unfolding as it should.

—MAX EHRMANN

However gradual the course of history, there must always be the day, even an hour and minute, when some significant action is performed for the first or last time.

—PETER QUENNELL

Life is a promise; fulfill it.

—MOTHER TERESA

Quality

There is one rule for the industrialist and that is: Make the best quality of goods possible at the lowest cost possible, paying the highest wages possible.

—HENRY FORD

Quality is never an accident; it is always the result of high intention, sincere effort, intelligent direction and skillful execution; it represents the wise choice of many alternatives.

—WILLIAM A. FOSTER

Just make up your mind at the very outset that your work is going to stand for quality … that you are going to stamp a superior quality upon everything that goes out of your hands, that whatever you do shall bear the hallmark of excellence.

—ORISON SWETT MARSDEN

Relationships

Treat people as if they were what they ought to be and you help them to become what they are capable of being.

—JOHANN WOLFGANG VON GOETHE

If we treat our employees correctly, they'll treat the customers right. And if customers are treated right, they'll come back.

—J. W. MARRIOTT JR.

A little reciprocity goes a long way.

—MALCOLM FORBES

Revolution

It is impossible to arouse the people artificially. People's revolutions are born from the course of events.

—MIKHAIL BAKUNIN

You can never have a revolution in order to establish a democracy. You must have a democracy in order to have a revolution.

—G. K. CHESTERTON

A nonviolent revolution is not a program of seizure of power. It is a program of transformation of relationships, ending in a peaceful transfer of power.

—MOHANDAS K. GANDHI

Risk

Don't be afraid to take a big step. You can't cross a chasm in two small jumps.

—DAVID LLOYD GEORGE

Being on a tightrope is living; everything else is waiting.

—KARL WALLENDA

There are two times in a man's life when he should not speculate: when he can't afford it and when he can.

—MARK TWAIN

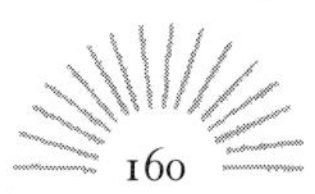

Sales

There is only one valid definition of business purpose: to create a customer.

—PETER DRUCKER

There is only one boss: the customer. And he can fire everybody in the company, from the chairman on down, simply by spending his money somewhere else.

—SAM WALTON

In every instance we found that the best-run companies stay as close to their customers as is humanly possible.

—THOMAS J. PETERS

A salesman is a fellow with a smile on his face, a shine on his shoes, and a lousy territory.

—GEORGE GOBEL

A thing is worth whatever the buyer will pay for it.

—PUBLILIUS SYRUS

People will buy anything that's one to a customer.

—SINCLAIR LEWIS

The only pretty store is one full of people.

—WILLIAM DILLARD

Customers don't want their money back; they want a product that works properly.

—DAN BURTON

Self-Confidence

Immense power is acquired by assuming yourself in your secret reveries that you were born to control affairs.

—ANDREW CARNEGIE

Attempt easy tasks as if they were difficult, and difficult as if they were easy; in the one case that confidence may not fall asleep, in the other that it may not be dismayed.

—BALTASAR GRACIAN

Our best friends and our worst enemies are our thoughts. A thought can do us more good than a doctor or a banker or a faithful friend. It can also do us more harm than a brick.

—DR. FRANK CRANE

As soon as you trust yourself, you will know how to live.

—JOHANN WOLFGANG VON GOETHE

It is best to act with confidence, no matter how little right you have to it.

—LILLIAN HELLMAN

Getting ahead in a difficult profession requires avid faith in yourself. That is why some people with mediocre talent, but with great inner drive, go much further than people with vastly superior talent.

—SOPHIA LOREN

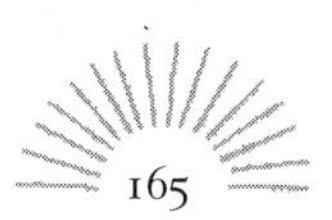

Self-Control

In the midst of movement and chaos, keep stillness inside of you.

—DEEPAK CHOPRA

He who restrains his anger overcomes his greatest enemy.

—LATIN PROVERB

There is only one corner of the universe you can be certain of improving and that's your own self.

—ALDOUS HUXLEY

Hot heads and cold hearts never solved anything.

—BILLY GRAHAM

Self-Esteem

No one can make you feel inferior without your consent.

—ELEANOR ROOSEVELT

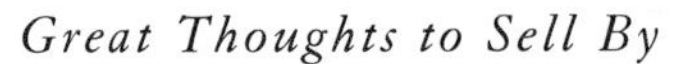

A man's head is his castle.

—JOSEPH HELLER

Outstanding leaders go out of the way to boost the self-esteem of their personnel.

—SAM WALTON

Self-esteem must be earned! When you dare to dream, dare to follow that dream, dare to suffer through the pain, sacrifice, self-doubts and friction from the world, you will genuinely impress yourself.

—DR. LAURA SCHLESSINGER

Self-esteem is as important to our well being as legs are to a table. It is essential for physical and mental health and for happiness.

—LOUISE HART

Selling

The human body has two ears and one mouth. To be good at persuading or selling, you must learn to use those natural devices in proportion. Listen twice as much as you talk and you'll succeed in persuading others nearly every time.

—TOM HOPKINS

If you would persuade, you must appeal to interest rather than intellect.

—BENJAMIN FRANKLIN

Everyone lives by selling something, whatever be his right to it.

—ROBERT LOUIS STEVENSON

The best way to get on in the world is to make people believe it's to their advantage to help you.

—JEAN DE LA BRUYÈRE

When a man is trying to sell you something, don't imagine he is that polite all the time.

—ED HOWE

Buying and selling; that's what the world has to go by.

—ANTHONY TROLLOPE

Silence

Don't talk unless you can improve the silence.

—NEW ENGLAND PROVERB

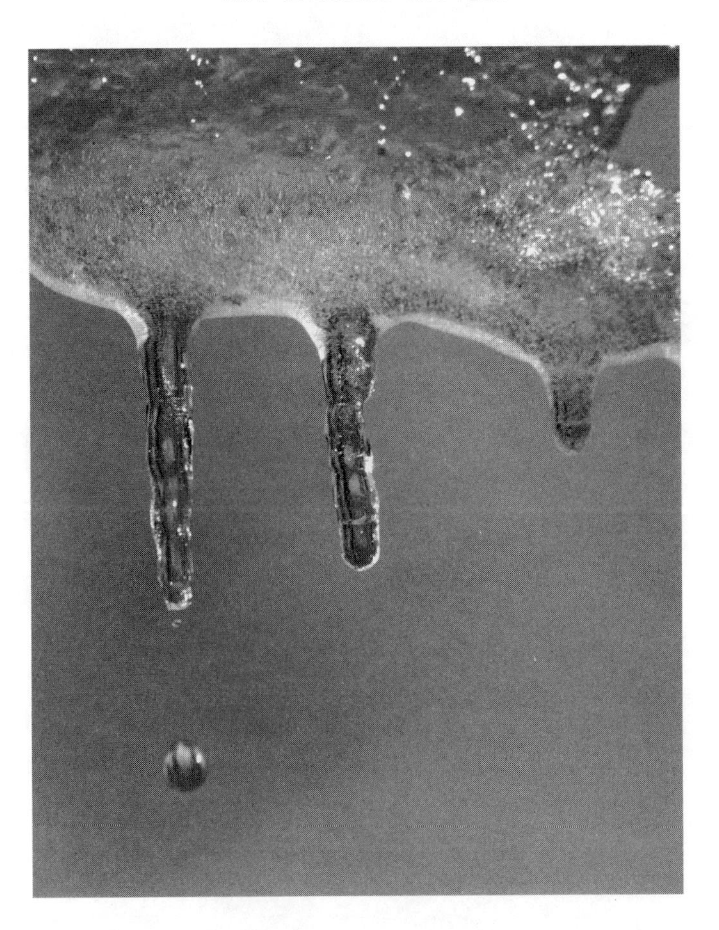

One often hears the remark "He talks too much," but when did anyone last hear the criticism "He listens too much?"

—NORMAN AUGUSTINE

It is impossible to persuade a man who does not disagree, but smiles.

—MURIEL SPARK

You have not converted a man because you have silenced him.

—JOHN MORLEY

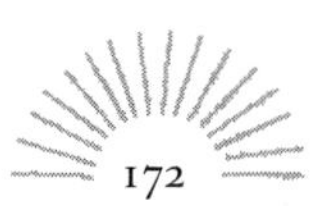

Too often the strong, silent man is silent because he does not know what to say.

—SIR WINSTON CHURCHILL

Look wise, say nothing, and grunt. Speech was given to conceal thoughts.

—SIR WILLIAM OSLER

Blessed is the man who, having nothing to say, abstains from giving in words evidence of the fact.

—GEORGE ELIOT

Sorrow

Although the world is very full of suffering, it is also full of the overcoming of it.

—HELEN KELLER

We are healed of suffering only by experiencing it to the full.

—MARCEL PROUST

The worse the news, the more effort should go into communicating it.

—ANDREW S. GROVE

A deep distress hath humanized my soul.

—WILLIAM WORDSWORTH

There are two days about which one should never worry, and these are yesterday and today.

—ROBERT JONES BURDETTE

We would often be sorry if our wishes were gratified.

—AESOP

The deeper that sorrow carves into your being, the more joy you can contain.

—KAHLIL GIBRAN

Find expression for a sorrow, and it will become dear to you. Find expression for a joy, and you will intensify its ecstasy.

—OSCAR WILDE

Success

You always pass failure on the way to success.

—MICKEY ROONEY

Many of life's failures are people who did not realize how close they were to success when they gave up.

—THOMAS EDISON

To succeed, jump as quickly at opportunities as you do at conclusions.

—BENJAMIN FRANKLIN

A person's probability of success is directly proportional to the belief and execution of their abilities.

—KENT CALHOUN

Success is not the result of spontaneous combustion. You must set yourself on fire.

—REGGIE LEACH

The most important single ingredient in the formula of success is knowing how to get along with people.

—THEODORE ROOSEVELT

The secret of success in life is for a man to be ready for his opportunity when it comes.

—BENJAMIN DISRAELI

The wise man puts all his eggs in one basket and watches the basket.

—ANDREW CARNEGIE

My formula for success? Rise early, work late, strike oil.

—J. PAUL GETTY

The man who will use his skill and constructive imagination to see how much he can give for a dollar instead of how little he can give for a dollar is bound to succeed.

—HENRY FORD

I know the price of success: dedication, hard work and an unremitting devotion to the things you want to see happen.

—FRANK LLOYD WRIGHT

The successful person is the individual who forms the habit of doing what the failing person doesn't like to do.

—DONALD RIGGS

Taxes

The hardest thing in the world to understand is income tax.

—ALBERT EINSTEIN

The avoidance of taxes is the only intellectual pursuit that still carries any reward.

—JOHN MAYNARD KEYNES

The art of taxation consists in so plucking the goose as to obtain the largest amount of feathers with the least possible amount of hissing.

—J. B. COLBERT

Simply by not owning three medium-sized castles in Tuscany I have saved enough money in the last forty years on insurance premiums alone to buy a medium-sized castle in Tuscany.

—LUDWIG MIES VAN DER ROHE

I don't want to tell you how much insurance I carry with the Prudential, but all I can say is, when I go, they go too.

—JACK BENNY

There is no such thing as a good tax.

—SIR WINSTON CHURCHILL

Thought

Man's great powers of thinking, remembering and communicating are responsible for the evolution of civilization.

—LINUS PAULING

The trouble with most people is that they think with their hopes or fears or wishes rather than with their minds.

—WILL DURANT

If thou thinkest twice before thou speakest once, thou wilt speak twice the better for it.

—WILLIAM PENN

The happiness of your life depends upon the quality of your thoughts … take care that you entertain no notions unsuitable to virtue and reasonable nature.

—MARCUS AURELIUS

If everyone is thinking alike, then somebody isn't thinking.

—GEORGE S. PATTON

Except our own thoughts, there is nothing absolutely in our power.

— RENÉ DESCARTES

It is the mark of an educated mind to be able to entertain a thought without accepting it.

—ARISTOTLE

If an idea's worth having once, it's worth having twice.

—TOM STOPPARD

Time Management

Don't duck the most difficult problems. That just ensures that the hardest part will be left when you're most tired. Get the big one done—it's down hill from there.

—NORMAN VINCENT PEALE

The secret of getting ahead is getting started. The secret of getting started is breaking your complex, overwhelming tasks into small manageable tasks, and then starting on the first one.

—MARK TWAIN

Time is a storm in which we are all lost.

—WILLIAM CARLOS WILLIAMS

Know the true value of time; snatch, seize, and enjoy every moment of it. No idleness, no laziness, no procrastination; never put off till tomorrow what you can do today.

—LORD CHESTERFIELD

Until we can manage time, we can manage nothing else.

—PETER DRUCKER

The more we do, the more we can do; the busier we are, the more leisure we have.

—WILLIAM HAZLITT

Doing the best at this moment puts you in the best place for the next moment.

—OPRAH WINFREY

Remember that time is money.

—BENJAMIN FRANKLIN

Toughness

Life is a grindstone. But whether it grinds you down or polishes you up depends upon what you are made of.

—ROBERT E. JOHNSON

You may not be responsible for getting knocked down, but you're certainly responsible for getting back up.

—REVEREND JESSE JACKSON

Determine that the thing can and shall be done, and then we shall find the way.

—ABRAHAM LINCOLN

When force is necessary, there it must be applied boldly, decisively and completely. But one must know the limitations of force; one must know when to blend force with a maneuver, the blow with an agreement.

—LEON TROTSKY

Truth

The truth exists; only fictions are invented.

—GEORGES BRAQUE

Truth never damages a cause that is just.

—MOHANDAS K. GANDHI

To know what people really think, pay regard to what they do, rather than what they say.

— RENÉ DESCARTES

Chase after truth like hell and you'll free yourself, even though you never touch its coattails.

—CLARENCE DARROW

The pursuit of truth and beauty is a sphere of activity in which we are permitted to remain children all our lives.

—ALBERT EINSTEIN

You shall know the truth, and the truth shall make you mad.

—ALDOUS HUXLEY

All great truths begin as blasphemies.

—GEORGE BERNARD SHAW

Truth has no special time of its own. Its hour is now—always.

—ALBERT SCHWEITZER

If you are out to describe the truth, leave elegance to the tailor.

—ALBERT EINSTEIN

Understanding

Understanding can overcome any situation, however mysterious or insurmountable it may appear to be.

—NORMAN VINCENT PEALE

Everything that irritates us about others can lead us to an understanding of ourselves.

—CARL JUNG

A process cannot be understood by stopping it. Understanding must move with the flow of the process, must join it and flow with it.

—FRANK HERBERT

Virtue

Recommend virtue to your children; it alone, not money, can make them happy. I speak from experience.

—LUDWIG VAN BEETHOVEN

Thinking is the hardest work there is, which is probably the reason why so few engage in it.

—HENRY FORD

I used to be Snow White, but I drifted.

—MAE WEST

To practice five things under all circumstances constitutes perfect virtue; these five are gravity, generosity of soul, sincerity, earnestness, and kindness.

—CONFUCIUS

The unfortunate thing about this world is that the good habits are much easier to give up than the bad ones.

—W. SOMERSET MAUGHAM

Virtue does not come from wealth, but wealth and every other good thing which men have comes from virtue.

—SOCRATES

Vision

Leaders must invoke an alchemy of great vision. Those leaders who do not are ultimately judged failures, even though they may be popular at the moment.

—HENRY KISSINGER

The reality is always there and is preceded by vision. And if one keeps looking steadily the vision crystallizes into fact or deed.

—HENRY MILLER

You need a well-articulated vision that people can follow.

—STEVEN P. JOBS

War and Peace

Aggression unopposed becomes a contagious disease.

—JIMMY CARTER

War may sometimes be a necessary evil. But no matter how necessary, it is always an evil, never a good. We will not learn how to live together in peace by killing each other's children.

—JIMMY CARTER

One is left with the horrible feeling now that war settles nothing; that to win a war is as disastrous as to lose one.

—AGATHA CHRISTIE

In times of peace the people look most to their representatives; but in war, to the executive solely.

—THOMAS JEFFERSON

If they want peace, nations should avoid the pinpricks that precede cannon shots.

—NAPOLEON BONAPARTE

Wealth

That some should be rich shows that others may become rich,
and hence is just encouragement to industry and enterprise.

—ABRAHAM LINCOLN

Money is applause.

—JACQUELINE SUSANN

I'm opposed to millionaires, but it would be dangerous to offer me the position.

—MARK TWAIN

I have been rich and I have been poor. Rich is better.

—SOPHIE TUCKER

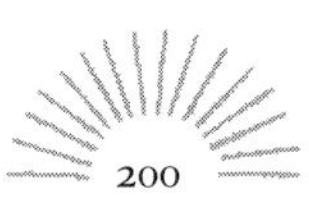

Mere moneymaking has never been my goal.

—JOHN D. ROCKEFELLER

Money remains the same, it is merely the pockets that change.

—GERTRUDE STEIN

Money never made a man happy yet, nor will it. There is nothing in its nature to produce happiness. The more a man has, the more he wants. Instead of filling a vacuum, it makes one.

—BENJAMIN FRANKLIN

The lack of money is the root of all evil.

—GEORGE BERNARD SHAW

Winning

I know the price of success: dedication, hard work and an unremitting devotion to the things you want to see happen.

—FRANK LLOYD WRIGHT

My philosophy of life is that if we make up our mind what we are going to make of our lives, then work hard toward that goal, we never lose—somehow we win out.

—RONALD REAGAN

Success seems to be connected with action. Successful people keep moving. They make mistakes, but they don't quit.

—CONRAD HILTON

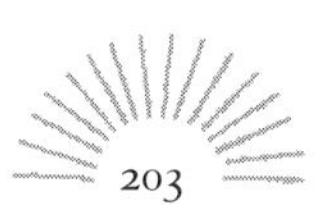

If anything goes bad, I did it. If anything goes semi-good, then we did it. If anything goes really good, then you did it. That's all it takes to get people to win football games.

—PAUL "BEAR" BRYANT

Wisdom

Our happiness depends on wisdom all the way.

—SOPHOCLES

The wisdom of the wise and the experience of the ages are perpetuated by quotations.

—BENJAMIN DISRAELI

Wisdom is the power to put our time and our knowledge to the proper use.

—THOMAS J. WATSON

The art of being wise is the art of knowing what to overlook.

—WILLIAM JAMES

It requires wisdom to understand wisdom: the music is nothing if the audience is deaf.

—WALTER LIPPMANN

Experiences are savings which a miser puts aside. Wisdom is an inheritance which a wastrel cannot exhaust.

—KARL KRAUS

A great memory is never made synonymous with wisdom, any more than a dictionary would be called a treatise.

—JOHN HENRY CARDINAL NEWMAN

Wisdom is like electricity. There is no permanently wise man, but men capable of wisdom, who, being put into certain company, or other favorable conditions, become wise for a short time, as glasses rubbed acquire electric power for a while.

—RALPH WALDO EMERSON

Work

I get quiet joy from the observation of anyone who does his job well.

—WILLIAM FEATHER

The closest to perfection a person comes is when he fills out a job application form.

—STANLEY J. RANDALL

Everybody looks good on paper.

—JOHN Y. BROWN, GOVERNOR OF KENTUCKY

A résumé is a balance sheet without any liabilities.

—ROBERT HALF

The reason that worry kills more people than work is that more people worry than work.

—ROBERT FROST

Some people work just hard enough not to get fired, and some companies pay people just enough that they won't quit.

—LOUIS E. BOONE

Always be smarter than the people who hire you.

—LENA HORNE

He started out at the bottom, and sort of likes it there.

—TENNESSEE ERNIE FORD

Writing

Composition is, for the most part, an effort of slow diligence and steady perseverance, to which the mind is dragged by necessity or resolution, and from which the attention is every moment starting to more delightful amusements.

—SAMUEL JOHNSON

Writing about an idea frees me of it. Thinking about it is a circle of repetitions.

—MASON COOLEY

No author is a man of genius to his publisher.

—HEINRICH HEINE

I took a course in speed-reading and was able to read *War and Peace* in twenty minutes. It's about Russia.

—WOODY ALLEN

Some books are to be tasted, others to be swallowed, and some few have to be chewed and digested.

—SIR FRANCIS BACON

I have always imagined that Paradise will be a kind of library.

—JORGE LUIS BORGES

News is the first rough draft of history.

—BENJAMIN BRADLEE

Zest

Wake up with a smile and go after life … Live it, enjoy it, taste it, smell it, feel it.

—JOE KNAPP

The only thing that keeps a man going is energy. And what is energy but liking life?

—LOUIS AUCHINCLOSS

Life engenders life. Energy creates energy. It is by spending oneself that one becomes rich.

—SARAH BERNHARDT

What hunger is in relation to food, zest is in relation to life.

—BERTRAND RUSSELL

What one has, one ought to use; and whatever he does, he should do with all his might.

—CICERO

What counts is not necessarily the size of the dog in the fight—it's the size of the fight in the dog.

—DWIGHT D. EISENHOWER

Security is mostly superstition … Life is either a daring adventure, or nothing.

—HELEN KELLER

Sometimes success is due less to ability than to zeal.

—CHARLES BRUXTON

INDEX OF AUTHORS

ABOUT THE AUTHOR

© Hisham Bharoocha

A dual citizen of both Austria and the United States, Gerhard Gschwandtner is the founder and publisher of *Selling Power*, the leading magazine for sales professionals worldwide, with a circulation of 165,000 subscribers in 67 countries.

He began his career in his native Austria in the sales training and marketing departments of a large construction equipment company. In 1972, he moved to the United States to become the company's North American Sales Training Director, later moving into the position of Marketing Manager.

In 1977, he became an independent sales training consultant, and in 1979 he created an audiovisual sales training course called "The Languages of Selling." Marketed to sales managers at Fortune 500 companies, the course taught nonverbal communication in sales together with professional selling skills.

In 1981, Gerhard launched *Personal Selling Power*, a tabloid-format newsletter directed to sales managers. Over the years the tabloid grew in subscriptions, size, and frequency. The name changed to *Selling Power*, and in magazine format it became the leader in the professional sales field. Every year *Selling Power* publishes the "Selling Power 500," a listing of the 500 largest sales forces in America. The company publishes books, sales training posters, and audio and video products for the professional sales market.

Gerhard has become America's leading expert on selling and sales management. He conducts webinars for such companies as SAP, and *Selling Power* has recently launched a new conference division that sponsors and conducts by-invitation-only leadership conferences directed toward companies with high sales volume and large sales forces.

For more information on *Selling Power* and its products and services, please visit www.sellingpower.com.